The Lord's Supper: The Church's Love Feast

By
Donald L. Norbie

WALTERICK PUBLISHERS
P.O. Box 2216
Kansas City, Kansas 66110

Printed in United States

Table of Contents

1

CONFUSION AT THE TABLE

Nearly 2000 years have passed since our Lord Jesus walked the dusty roads of Galilee. His life, death, and resurrection are ancient history; and the primeval days of the Church are shrouded by antiquity.

Today the original unified church has shattered into countless fragments. The Eastern and Western Churches divided rather early, the West unifying under the Bishop of Rome. For a thousand years this unity was maintained with an iron hand by the Pope.

But the Reformation shattered this monolith as Martin Luther and others rained blow after blow upon the structure. Since then division has marked Christendom, with the various Protestant churches continuing to divide over structure, doctrine, or charismatic leaders.

The teaching and practice of the Lord's Supper has not escaped attack. Attend a church on Sunday when the congregation is observing communion and you will sense immediately great differences in the way the service is conducted.

Some will have an altar and a railing to guard it from the laity. Here the priest or minister officiates in his flowing robes. Those who participate come forward, kneel, and partake of the wafer. In some churches the priest alone drinks from the cup; in others, the laity also partake. There is a sense of mystery here. Some churches teach that the body of Christ is offered afresh, a new sacrifice is made.

Visit another church and you will see no altar or railing. A table is placed at the front and a minister officiates. After Scripture is read and prayer offered, the bread and cup (or cups) are passed around through the congregation. All who wish partake. This ceremony is often appended to the regular preaching service as a sort of postscript. Here the atmosphere is more casual, rather like looking at the picture of a famous ancestor.

Again, you might visit another group seated in rows or in a large circle around the table. The bread and cup are there. The scene is starkly simple, a determined effort to focus on the bread and the red-filled cup. Here no minister presides. Various men arise in a spontaneous manner to pray, announce a hymn, or speak from the Word. There is no brief or hurried ceremony but a prolonged period of an hour or more which focuses on worship and praise to the Lord. It is not a liturgical service yet may be marked by deep, quiet emotion and intense reverence.

Quite different, aren't they? There are a host of variations even on the above models. The Church seems a little confused at the table! What does this service represent and how should it be observed? Or does it matter? What does it all mean and does Scripture give any guidelines?

Perhaps you yourself are perplexed. It is the purpose of this study to examine Scripture and to clarify thinking. It is also the longing of the author that each one may come to appreciate this memorial service in a new way and to know his love for the Lord deepened as he remembers Christ's death.

2

DESCRIPTIVE NAMES

The names we give celebrations have real significance. A date may recall a special event such as the "Fourth of July." The name may indicate the purpose, such as "Memorial Day" or "Mother's Day."

What names are used in the New Testament for this frequent time of remembrance?

The night before Christ's betrayal and crucifixion He met with His disciples for the Passover. (There is some question about the day but the best evidence is for Thursday and that it was a Passover meal–cf. **"Dictionary of New Testament Theology,"** Vol. 2, p. 527; **"The New Bible Dictionary,"** p. 748.) Matthew tells us, "Now when evening had come, He was reclining at the table with the twelve disciples" (Matt. 26:20, New American Standard Bible. All Bible references will be from this version.) The observance was early called "the Lord's Supper" by the churches (1 Cor. 11:20). This is still a common designation by Protestant churches.

It seems as if the most common name then was "the breaking of bread." Although the expression was used in a general way of eating (Acts 27:35), at times it clearly reveals a specialized use for the Lord's Supper (Acts 2:42; 20:7). A prominent activity in the Supper thus became its designation.

Because a meal often accompanied this "breaking of bread," it was described by Jude as a "love feast" (Jude 12). This was a time of meditation, of luxuriating in the warmth of God's love. Because of this, love flowed freely between all of God's family present. A love feast! It should be that today.

Some today call it a "remembrance feast." According to Paul, the Lord said, "This do in remembrance of me" (1 Cor. 11:24). The term does emphasize the purpose of such a time. Moses warned Israel before he died, "Watch yourself lest you forget the Lord who brought you from the land of Egypt, out of the house of slavery" (Deut. 6:12). The Lord Jesus pleads today, "Remember me!"

The term "communion" is used by some churches. Many today do not know the origin of the term nor its significance. To them it may only mean a mystical ceremony. But it is a good term with deep Scriptural roots. Man has been estranged and separated from his Maker. Now through Christ's death he can "commune" or "share" with God. Where there was once alienation there is now communion, *koinonia* (1 Cor. 10:16, Greek).

Some try to make a distinction between the Lord's table in 1 Corinthians 10:21 and the Lord's supper in 1 Corinthians 11:20. It is an artificial distinction which cannot be sustained. The heathen sat down to eat with their gods in heathen feasts. The believer sits at the Lord's table and partakes of the Lord's supper, proclaiming he is in fellowship with his God. Communion is a good term when understood correctly.

The terms "breaking of bread" and "Lord's supper" were the common terms used in the first century. Others were added later. The word "eucharist" (Greek—thanksgiving) appeared in the second century. The "mass" (from *missio*, "a sending away," because non-members were dismissed) is a later term. Martin Luther called the Lord's Supper the "Sacrament of the Altar" in his Small Catechism.

Today churches which strive for New Testament simplicity often use the terms "Breaking of Bread" or "Lord's Supper." The Lord's Supper is probably the most common term used by most evangelical Christians and communicates well to all.

3

THE PASSOVER SETTING

For months Jesus had warned His disciples of His coming death. After Peter's exciting confession, "Thou art the Christ, the Son of the Living God" (Matt. 16:16), Jesus pronounced him blessed. God had given Peter spiritual insight. Then Christ began to speak in a somber tone of His coming suffering, "that He must go to Jerusalem and suffer many things from the elders and chief priests and scribes, and be killed, and be raised up on the third day" (Matt. 16:21).

Peter rebuked Jesus for such a prediction and was himself rebuked by the Master. The suffering and cross were a vital part of Christ's mission. This was difficult for the disciples to accept. They wanted a triumphant, conquering Messiah.

As opposition to Him mounted during the last year of His ministry Jesus spoke increasingly of His coming death (Matt. 20:17-19). He told parables also which graphically portrayed His rejection and death (Matt. 21:33-40).

It was the year A.D. 30 and Jesus had come with His disciples to Jerusalem for the Passover. There was a triumphal entry into the city with teeming, shouting crowds accompanying Him. This was followed by daily teaching in the temple. Evenings He and His disciples would leave the city, descend to the Kidron Valley, and then wend their way up the Mount of Olives and stay in Bethany. Mary and Martha's home was a safe sanctuary for Him, a refuge from the vicious hatred He sensed in Jerusalem.

On Thursday, the first day of the Feast of Unleavened Bread, the disciples asked Him, "Where do you want us to prepare for you to eat the Passover?" (Matt. 26:17). He gave them instructions on how to find a certain house where they would be welcomed and could make ready. "And the disciples did as Jesus had directed them; and they prepared the Passover" (Matt. 26:19).

From other sources we know the established order used in the first century for the Passover. The general instructions of Exodus 12 had been stylized over the centuries into a meaningful ritual (**"New International Dictionary of the New Testament,"** Vol. II, p. 522).

First, the head of the household pronounced the prayer of sanctification, asking God to bless the festival and the first cup of wine. This was followed by a course of green herbs, bitter herbs, and a sauce of fruit juice.

The meal was then brought in and the household head went over the Passover liturgy. He explained the main features of the meal (Exod. 12:26) and told the moving story of Israel's redemption from Egypt. Then the family would sing the first Hallel (Psa. 113, 114) and the second cup, mixed with water, was drunk.

A prayer was then offered over the unleavened bread and this was distributed. The main meal was eaten, consisting of lamb, unleavened bread, and bitter herbs. Following this another prayer was offered over the third cup, called the cup of blessing, and this was passed to each member.

The second part of the Hallel (Psa. 115—118) was then sung and the fourth cup was passed (the Hallel cup) after a benediction. The service was thus completed.

This was likely the order Jesus followed as He met with His disciples. He presided as the head of their household and it was a moving occasion. As He recited the story of Israel's redemption from Egypt following the slaughter of the lamb, He was deeply moved by thoughts of His own impending death. Years before John had announced Him as the Lamb of God (John 1:29). Shortly now as God's Lamb He would be slaughtered and His blood would flow.

Jehovah had instituted the Passover Feast as a remembrance for Israel to remind them of His great love and their deliverance from slavery. Now Christ instituted a remembrance ritual to commemorate His deliverance of mankind from the bondage of sin.

As the unleavened bread was passed, Jesus startled His disciples by saying, "Take, eat; this is My body" (Matt. 26:26). No longer was the unleavened bread to be a reminder of the hurried flight from Egypt by Israel. The loaf would symbolize His body soon to be mutilated on the cross.

Later the third cup was passed after prayer. Ah, to have been there and heard that prayer! As Jesus' hand passed the cup He said solemnly, "Drink from it, all of you; for this is My blood of the covenant which is poured out for many for forgiveness of sins" (Matt. 26:27,28).

The little band of shaken disciples sang the last Hallel, drank the fourth cup, and went out into a forbiddingly dark night. As they made their way through the city streets, out the gate, and down into the Kidron Valley their thoughts were very confused. What did all this mean?

4

FIRST CENTURY PRACTICE

After forty days of proving His resurrection by repeated appearances to His disciples (Acts 1:3), the Lord Jesus went back to heaven in a blaze of glory. The disciples gazed heavenward in rapt attention until the angels brought them back to earth by saying, "Men of Galilee, why do you stand looking into the sky? This Jesus, who has been taken up from you into heaven will come in just the same way as you have watched Him go into heaven" (Acts 1:11).

They returned to Jerusalem to await the coming of the Holy Spirit as they had been instructed by their Lord (Acts 1:8). They desperately needed divine power to fulfill their mission, this little band of timid disciples. Jesus had said their mission was to spread the message of forgiveness through faith in Him, in His death and resurrection. It was an impossible task, humanly speaking.

Fifty days after Passover was the Jewish Feast of Pentecost, also called the "feast of weeks" since seven weeks had elapsed (Exod. 34:22). It marked the completion of barley harvest and was also called the "day of firstfruits" (Exod. 23:16). This was one of three annual festivals on which every Jewish male was expected to be in Jerusalem (Deut. 16:16). At Pentecost, Jerusalem was teeming with excited Jewish men from all over the Roman Empire, come to worship.

The band of disciples, 120 strong, men and women, continued praying and waiting for God to work (Acts 1:14-15). On the Day of Pentecost there was suddenly the sound of a rushing, roaring wind in the room. Tongues of fire came down and rested on the disciples; the room exploded with exuberant joy and praise—in languages they had never learned.

As they spilled out of the room into the street, a great crowd gathered, amazed by their enthusiasm and their fluency in foreign languages. People from the limits of the known world heard provincial Galileans speaking fluently in languages they had never studied (Acts 2:11). This was not an ecstatic mouthing of nonsense syllables but current spoken languages. No wonder the crowd was amazed.

Peter seizes the occasion to address the crowd and preaches powerfully, proclaiming Jesus whom they had rejected and crucified to be the true Messiah, the hope of Israel. Powerful witness was given to the resurrection, God's validation of Jesus' Messianic claims. The crowd was moved and pierced by conviction and guilt. They cried to Peter, "What shall we do?" (Acts 2:37). They were told to repent and to show their acceptance of Jesus by baptism.

It was a great day, the beginning of the New Testament Church. Three thousand professed faith in Christ and were baptized. The Apostles quickly took leadership and began teaching these new converts. There was much they had to learn.

The program of the Church was simple: "the apostles' teaching," "fellowship" (sharing and interaction as a congregation), "breaking bread" (Lord's Supper), and "prayer" (Acts 2:42). Although breaking bread was a term used at times for an ordinary meal, here it is likened with the Church's congregational activity and must refer to the Lord's Supper, the remembrance of Christ's death (**"International Standard Bible Encyclopaedia,"** Vol. III, p. 1923).

Thus, right from the beginning the Church took seriously the Lord's plea to remember His death. It was interwoven into the basic pattern of the fabric of their meeting. As the message spread and churches were formed, the universal practice was to meet for teaching, fellowship, "breaking of bread," and prayer. At first the celebration may have been fairly often but in time it became a weekly,

Sunday meeting. Paul waited in Troas a week, knowing on Sunday the church would gather "to break bread" (Acts 20:6-7). The custom is indicated by this offhand reference.

That this practice continued is reflected in the *Didache,* a document from the early church (ca. 125 A.D.). "But on the Lord's day do assemble and break bread, and give thanks, after confessing your transgressions, in order that your sacrifice may be pure" (ch. 14).

But how was the service conducted? And here we must beware of reading current practice back into the first century. Paul would probably hardly recognize the Lord's Supper as practiced by some today.

It is Paul who draws aside the curtain of silence and gives us a glimpse into a first century church meeting, the assembly at Corinth. The Christians apparently gathered for a meal at the conclusion of which they passed the loaf and cup and remembered Christ's death for them. In 1 Corinthians 11 Paul seeks to correct certain abuses which had crept into their practice. As he deals with these abuses, he also gives positive instruction for their meetings.

One area of confusion was concerning the roles of the sexes. Although Paul affirms that in our spiritual relationship with Christ "there is neither male nor female" (Gal. 3:28), yet in this life and in the churches sexual differences are to be observed. The differences apply to dress (1 Cor. 11:4, 5) and to role (1 Cor. 11:3). Paul believed strongly in masculine leadership and pleaded the universal practice of the churches (1 Cor. 11:16; 14:33,34).

The church in Corinth was guilty of intemperance at the meal both in food and drink. There was also a failure to share. Some went hungry (1 Cor. 11:21). Paul urges, therefore, if one is hungry he should eat at home (1 Cor. 11:22). The purpose in coming together should be to remember Christ's death, not to eat food. Because of this admonition, in time the fellowship meal seems to have been discontinued.

There should be a spirit of reverence at the meeting. Sin and the spirit of division must be judged before eating the loaf and drinking the cup (1 Cor. 11:28). Sin and irreverence will be judged by God. It is a solemn thing to worship the One Who is holy.

Evidently the Lord's words were repeated and they broke the bread and passed it: "This is My body, which is for you; this do in remembrance of Me." The cup was then passed, remembering the words, "This cup is the new covenant in My blood; do this as often as you drink it in remembrance of Me" (1 Cor. 11:24,25).

But what structure was there in the meeting? Which liturgy was used? Who was in charge?

Here again the letter to the Corinthians gives insight. Elders as the spiritual leaders of the flock were to lead and to guard against disorder and abuse (Tit. 1:9-11). But there seemed to be no rigid order of service, no iron-bound program. The Spirit of God was allowed much liberty. Did not Paul write, "Do not quench the Spirit" (1 Thess. 5:19)?

"What is the outcome then, brethren? When you assemble, each one has a psalm, has a teaching, has a revelation, has a tongue, has an interpretation. Let all things be done for edification" (1 Cor. 14:26).

The atmosphere of the meeting was one of freedom and joy. There was no clergy-laity distinction. All functioned as priests and each could exercise his gift. There was no specified order. But during the meeting there was a point when prayer was offered and the loaf and cup were passed. All remembered anew the agonizing death of their Savior and their love was kindled afresh for Him.

From Corinth we see how a New Testament church functioned. But was Corinth an exception, an aberration? Not according to Paul! He claims the sanction for his instruction from the universal practice of the churches—"as in all the churches of the saints" (1 Cor. 14:33b). Evidently, while there was much liberty, there were certain principles laid down by the Apostles to govern the churches in their functioning.

5

HISTORY BRINGS CHANGES

The Apostolic Age ended with the death of John (ca. 90 A.D.). As the second century began, the apostolic tradition was still strong. The *Didache* reveals conformity to the New Testament writings in its teaching and exhortations. The churches were still marked by simplicity and enthusiasm.

But the passing of time saw an erosion of this simplicity and truth. The strident voice of Ignatius (d. 117 A.D.) was raised, demanding that one elder be chosen as bishop over the other elders. A plurality of leadership was seen as leading to weakness and indecisiveness. This movement accelerated until by the end of the second century most churches were led by a bishop.

This was accompanied by the development of the clergy as special mediators of the grace of God and instructors of the flock. Spontaneous worship became structured and was led by the bishop and elders. The priesthood of all believers was a doctrine no longer taught nor practiced. Ignatius early cried out for the bishop's unique authority: "It is not lawful without the bishop either to baptize or to make an agape" (Epistle to the Magnesians).

The Eucharist, as it was increasingly called, became more and more a mystical observance. "The public service was divided from the middle of the second century down to the close of the fifth, into the worship of the catechumens and the worship of the faithful" (Schaff, **"History of the Christian Church,"** Vol. II, p. 232). The first service was open to the unbaptized and consisted of songs, prayers, and preaching. These were then dismissed (*missa,* from which mass is derived) and the faithful remained to celebrate the Lord's Supper. The mysteries of baptism and the Eucharist were for the initiated only.

By the second century the agape (fellowship meal) became separated from the Lord's Supper. The service consisted usually of two parts: the oblation or presenting of the offering of the congregation followed by the communion, the partaking of the bread and cup. All members partook of both elements.

Irenaeus states that the bread and wine become the body and blood of the Lord by the power of the Holy Spirit. Yet he guards this statement by also speaking of them as "antitypes," emphasizing they are distinct from the literal body and blood of Christ (Schaff, Vol. II, p. 242). The Eucharist was viewed as a commemoration of Christ's completed sacrifice, not as another sacrifice for sin.

As time passed there was an increasing inclination toward the concept of transubstantiation, that the bread and wine become literally the body and blood of our Lord. There was also a drift toward the Greek and the Roman idea of the Eucharist as a sacrifice. But some like Athanasius insisted on only a spiritual participation and that the elements were simply symbols (Schaff, Vol. III, p. 496), as did Cyprian and Tertullian.

This was the age of the papacy asserting its power. Leo I, the Great (440–461), was, strictly speaking, the first pope. He was the first bishop of Rome to develop the doctrine of the papacy and to insist on his authority over the whole church. "He was animated with the unwavering conviction that the Lord himself had committed to him, as the successor of Peter, the care of the whole church" (Schaff, Vol. III, p. 317). In the midst of great political turmoil and confusion Leo emerged as a rock of stability and authority. The papacy became firmly entrenched.

During the Middle Ages the doctrine of transubstantiation gained increasing acceptance. The priest was viewed as offering the sacrifice of Christ's literal body and blood in the sacrament. The power of the priests grew and an air of mystery surrounded the Mass. This was true of both the Eastern and Western Churches.

A French monk, Paschasius Radbertus (800–865), was the first to teach clearly the doctrine of transubstantiation as it was later accepted by the Roman Catholic Church. He taught that "the substance of bread and wine is effectually changed . . . into the flesh and blood of Christ." After the priestly consecration there is "nothing else in the eucharist but the flesh and blood of Christ" (Schaff, Vol. IV, p. 547).

His writings influenced many and were ultimately to prevail, although opposed by some. Ratramnus, a contemporary French monk, contended that the bread and wine were only figures and pledges of Christ's body and blood. They were still literally bread and wine. The value was in the spiritual significance to the believer's mind. Radbertus was ultimately canonized and Ratramnus was condemned. Transubstantiation became the accepted doctrine of Roman Catholicism after 1050 A.D. The Council of Trent (1545–1563) confirmed this.

Accompanying this was the withdrawal of the communion cup from the laity. There was a superstitious fear of spilling the blood of Christ. This further strengthened the power of the priesthood over the laity (Schaff, Vol. IV, p. 569). The sacrifice of Calvary was repeated at every Mass. The priest's power indeed was awesome!

With the attacks of Martin Luther and the ensuing Reformation, the monolithic authority of Rome was shattered. Doctrines were questioned and restated. The selling of indulgences was only the first of many doctrines to be challenged by the Reformers. Transubstantiation too knew the critique of Scripture. All things were subject to evaluation by the Word of God. The fear of excommunication by Rome was gone.

Martin Luther wrote **"The Babylonian Captivity of the Church"** in which he accused Rome of taking the Church into captivity. One form of captivity was the denial of the cup to the laity. Another bondage was the doctrine of transubstantiation. Luther believed the elements were real bread and wine, not changed in their essence. A third bondage was the teaching that the Mass is a good work and a sacrifice. For Luther it was a reminder of God's gift to us, not a sacrifice to God (Latourette, **"A History of Christianity,"** p. 712).

Other reformers attacked the doctrine of transubstantiation as well. Although unfortunately they did not agree among themselves as to the true significance of the Lord's Supper, they were unanimous in opposing Rome. The Lord's Supper was not a sacrifice offered to God to atone for sin but a memorial of God's gift to man, Christ's once-for-all sacrifice on the cross for sin.

> Done is the work that saves!
> Once and forever done;
> Finished the righteousness
> That clothes the unrighteous one;
> The love that blesses us below,
> Is flowing freely to us now.
> —Horatius Bonar

6

CURRENT VIEWS

One could long for the simplicity of the Apostolic Church before centuries of theological argument divided the churches. The Lord's Supper has not escaped controversy by theologians.

During the first century it was viewed as a remembrance time for the Church even as Passover was a remembrance for Israel. The various parts of the Passover meal when accompanied by the Scripture and a retelling of those ancient events stirred Israel afresh. Their imaginations came alive with scenes of slavery, of the plagues poured out on Egypt, of a lamb slaughtered and blood applied to the door posts, of family units clustered around tables eating the lamb.

These tangible objects brought back a flood of memories to the devout Israelites. God had punished Egypt and delivered them. God had led them through the desert and into the promised land. Jehovah was their God and they were His people. Joy and praise filled their hearts.

There is no suggestion that any Israelite ever viewed the Passover as a sacrament, conferring some grace upon the participants. To them it was a meal, food, nothing more. It was the father's retelling of history that made the rite come alive.

As Jesus sat at that last Passover, the parallels were very clear to Him. The world was in slavery to sin (John 8:34). As the lamb was slain in Egypt to avert judgment, so He would die for the sins of the people (John 1:29). God's lamb must suffer and die.

The Lord had asked Israel never to forget their deliverance. For over 1400 years the Jews had remembered that historic event annually. Now Jesus is concerned for the future of His Church. His death must never be forgotten. It is the basis of all forgiveness and hope. He takes two simple elements, bread and wine, to picture His body and blood. The blood and body separated graphically portray a violent death. The bread broken by each reminds the eater of a body mutilated on the cross. The Scripture read and the event retold keep the memory of the cross alive.

Symbols! As the bitter herbs and lamb were eaten it was a time of recounting their history. "And it will come about when your children will say to you, 'What does this rite mean to you?' that you shall say, 'It is a Passover. . . .' " The symbols prompted the word and the word gave significance to the rite. The same should be true today of the Lord's Supper. Divorced from the word and an active remembering of the historic event, it becomes a meaningless ritual.

We have traced the historic evolution of a simple remembrance rite into an ornate sacrament filled with mystery and awe. There is magic in the service. Under the hands of the priest the earthly bread and wine are transformed into the physical body and blood of our Lord. Mysterious alchemy of heaven! The sacrifice of the cross is repeated before the wondering eyes of the worshipers. To partake of the bread now is to partake physically of Christ and to know an infusion of grace enabling one to live a holy life. Symbol has become sacrament. This is still Rome's stand.

Thomas Aquinas wrote:
"Hear what holy Church maintaineth,
That the bread its substance changeth
Into Flesh, the wine to Blood.
Doth it pass thy comprehending?
Faith, the law of sight transcending
Leaps to things not understood."

(Schaff, Vol. IV, p. 571)

During the Reformation the doctrines held by Rome came under attack. Martin Luther rejected transubstantiation (the change of substance) but then advanced his own view, which has a tinge of mystery.

In the words of his Small Catechism: "What is the Sacrament of the Altar? It is the true Body and Blood of our Lord Jesus Christ, under the bread and wine, given unto us Christians to eat and to drink, as it was instituted by Christ Himself." He further states, "The words, 'This is my body' and 'This is my blood,' teach us that the body and blood of Christ are truly present in the Lord's Supper."

The Lord's Supper thus is a sacrament. "A sacrament is a holy ordinance instituted by Christ Himself, in which through earthly means we receive heavenly gifts of grace." Thus Luther could say, " 'Given and shed for you for the remission of sins'. . . . Through these words the remission of sins, life and salvation are given unto us in the Sacrament."

Luther's view has been called "consubstantiation." The elements are not changed but the true body and blood are present with them. Do not ask Luther to explain this! You must accept it by faith. The air of mystery surrounding the Mass is carried over into Luther's Communion. It too is a sacrament conferring grace, although not a sacrifice.

Zwingli (1484–1531) was an early Swiss reformer, a contemporary of Luther. His break with Rome was more thorough and complete than Luther's. When he and Luther discussed the meaning of the Lord's Supper Luther stressed "This is my body" and took the statement at face value. Christ's body must be actually present.

Zwingli, on the other hand, emphasized, "Do this in memory of me." To him it was a symbol, a memorial. Luther clung persistently to his view, a view which Zwingli regarded as a remnant of Roman Catholic superstition. So the two men parted, unable to work together, a tragedy for the Church.

John Calvin (1509–1564) was a reformer who had tremendous influence in forming the thinking of the Reformation. He wrote voluminously. His views on the Lord's Supper mediate between Zwingli and Luther.

Calvin disagreed with Luther that the physical body of Christ was present with the bread; but he felt it was more than a memorial or a sign, as Zwingli held. To Calvin, Christ was truly present with the bread, although in a spiritual sense. The sacrament is a marvelous means of grace to the believer through his mystical union with Christ. Calvin wrote, "And first we are not to dream of such a presence of Christ in the sacrament as the artificers of the Romish court have imagined, as if the body of Christ, locally present, were to be taken into the hand, and chewed by the teeth, and swallowed by the throat" (Calvin, **"Institutes of the Christian Religion,"** Vol. II, p. 564). Calvin denounced transubstantiation very strongly.

Calvin states his own position as "too high a mystery either for my mind to comprehend or my words to express; and to speak more plainly, I rather feel than understand it. . . . In his sacred Supper he bids me take, eat, and drink his body and blood under the symbols of bread and wine. I have no doubt that He will truly give and I receive" (**"Institutes,"** Vol. II, p. 587).

For Calvin there was a mystical spiritual feeding on Christ that especially accompanied the Lord's Supper, although Christ's physical body was truly in heaven. Calvin was a very logical man, very cerebral in his approach, but here he confessed to feeling, rather than understanding.

The Quakers go to the extreme of rejecting the observance completely. All is spiritualized and no symbols are used.

Today these varied schools of thought still flourish. The Roman Catholic and Greek Churches hold to transubstantiation. Multitudes are enthralled by the pageantry of the Mass as the priest performs divine alchemy and the elements change under his hand into the physical body and blood of Christ. The sacrifice of the cross is repeated afresh.

Lutherans still believe in consubstantiation and believe that the real body and blood of Christ are present with the physical bread and wine. Faith is required to believe this.

The Presbyterian and Reformed Churches often hold Calvin's view that the mystical body of Christ is truly present and is eaten at the Supper. Calvin confessed this was a mystery to him.

The view which Zwingli and others taught is widely held by many evangelicals today. The elements are simply signs and symbols. As the Passover was rich with symbolism, recalling the exciting events of the exodus from Egypt, so the symbols of the loaf and cup recall the suffering and dying of Christ to the believer. This is no sacrament with an air of mystery and with divine grace flowing through the elements. It is a no-nonsense approach; the only blessing will come from the worshiper's hearing the Word and thinking, remembering, and worshiping.

When Christ said, "This is my body," He meant, "This *represents* my body." Both from Scripture and from experience this is the truest understanding of His words.

Undoubtedly the ritual of the Mass with its rich color, pageantry, and fragrant incense is an emotionally exciting experience. But fleshly emotion is not the same as spiritual edification. It is the Word and meditation that produce true edification, not simply the bread between the teeth.

> Only bread and only wine
> Yet to faith the solemn sign
> Of the heavenly and divine!
> We give Thee thanks, O Lord.
>
> For the words that turn our eye
> To the cross of Calvary,
> Bidding us in faith draw nigh,
> We give Thee thanks, O Lord.
> —Horatius Bonar

7

PRIESTS AT WORSHIP

The children of Israel had a limited priesthood. It was the tribe of Levi that had the privilege of ministry in the tabernacle and later in the temple, and from the tribe of Levi one family was chosen to have an hereditary priesthood.

God said, "And I will consecrate the tent of meeting and the altar; I will also consecrate Aaron and his sons to minister as priests to Me" (Exod. 29:44). The priests offered the sacrifices and ministered in holy things, assisted by the Levites. They could enter the Holy Place, an area forbidden to the ordinary Israelite. Into the Holy of Holies only the High Priest entered and that on one day of the year, the Day of Atonement.

God was holy, altogether "other," majestic, and awesome. The sinfulness of man and his alienation were emphasized in tabernacle worship. Blood sacrifice was the only remedy for man's sin and separation, but even with that he stood afar off and worshiped. Sin was not completely dealt with yet.

But the book of Hebrews proclaims that the old has passed away and a new covenant has been inaugurated. ". . . He is also the mediator of a better covenant, which has been enacted on better promises" (Heb. 8:6). He, as High Priest, offered Himself to God as a sacrifice for sins—". . . this He did once for all when He offered up Himself" (Heb. 7:27).

Those who are of the new covenant by faith in Jesus Christ have a place of nearness. Sin has been forever taken away and there is a joy and liberty unknown before.

> No blood, no altar now,
> The sacrifice is o'er!
> No flame, no smoke ascends on high,
> The lamb is slain no more,
> But richer blood has flowed from nobler veins,
> To purge the soul from guilt
> And cleanse the reddest stains.
> —Horatius Bonar

The believer now is invited as a priest to draw near. This privilege is not reserved for an elite class but is the right of every child of God. Does not Peter say of all Christians, "But you are a chosen race, a royal priesthood, a holy nation, a people for God's own possession. . . ." (1 Pet. 2:9).

With this in mind the writer of Hebrews states:

> ". . . we have confidence to enter the holy place by the blood of Jesus" (Heb. 10:19).
> "And since we have a great priest over the house of God, let us draw near with a sincere heart in full assurance of faith. . . ." (Heb. 10:21–22).

Who then should participate at the Lord's Supper? Certainly only those can enter into the spirit of the remembrance time who have come to know God's grace and received Christ as Lord and Savior. One can only remember what he has experienced.

The tragedy of many churches is that pews are filled with unregenerate, baptized, church members who woodenly partake of the elements when they are passed. By so doing, many feel they earn favor with God and merit heaven. What was to be a memorial of God's grace has become a work to earn heaven!

Acts tells us the sequence of events on the Day of Pentecost. People received the word preached, a message of repentance and faith in Christ. These were intelligent, mature persons who could understand and choose.

Following this they were baptized and joined ranks with the disciples (Acts 2:41). It was then they entered into the program of the church: teaching, fellowship, breaking of bread, and prayer (Acts 2:42). The church had the opportunity to screen and to evaluate those who would join its ranks.

Churches need to do the same today. A person desiring fellowship should know the Gospel and be able to give an account of his own conversion. Baptism should be encouraged for young converts as a proclamation of faith. Because of confusion in teaching on baptism some who come to know the Lord may cling to their earlier baptism as adequate. Elders of an assembly may lovingly welcome such and seek to teach them further, rather than turn them away. Love will accept all of God's children, regardless of their imperfect understanding.

"Wherefore, accept one another, just as Christ also accepted us to the glory of God" (Rom. 15:7).

How often should this memorial feast be conducted? Churches vary here. Some have the Lord's Supper quarterly, others monthly or weekly. Often the statement is made, "Well, Jesus said as often as you do it. He did not give any frequency."

True. But does not the example of the Apostolic Church carry any weight? Bible scholars agree that the early Christians observed the Lord's Supper at least weekly (Acts 20:7). The post-apostolic church has a unanimous witness to the importance and frequency of the rite. Christians can hardly claim to be a New Testament church if they do not remember Christ's death weekly. The frequency does not jade the experience if the heart is filled with love for Christ.

> To Calvary, Lord, in spirit now,
> Our grateful souls repair,
> To dwell upon Thy dying love,
> And taste its sweetness there.
> —Edward Denny

What are the elements to be used? If this is a sacrament with mysterious grace flowing through the bread and wine, then the composition of the elements may be vital. Perhaps God's grace can only be mediated through fermented wine and unleavened bread. And most scholars would agree these were the elements Jesus took in His hands.

But if it is a symbol, then the exact chemical composition of the bread and wine are less vital. Whether it be wheat, rye, corn, or rice flour matters little. The mind can still reflect on Christ. Whether it be wine (and wine can look blood-red), grape juice, or some other available liquid is not that crucial. The vital activity takes place in the believer's mind and heart, not on the table.

Should it be one loaf or crackers? Here Paul does make a point. The one loaf pictures both Christ's physical body and His mystical body, the Church. "Since there is one bread (loaf), we who are many are one body; for we all partake of the one bread" (1 Cor. 10:17). The symbolism of the one loaf, the unity of Christ's body is important.

Should there be one cup or more? When a group is very small one cup may be adequate. As the fellowship grows there may be two or four. Some may go to small individual cups. Who has a right to judge here? The wine is liquid and does not picture unity in the same way as the loaf. We may have our preference, but let us be careful in judging others.

What should be the mode of our meeting? Here 1 Corinthians 14 certainly indicates an openness, an opportunity for a number to participate. This is a powerful proclamation of the priesthood of all believers. There is no liturgy or order of service but opportunity for the Spirit to direct in hymns, prayers, and Scriptures read. When the bread is broken and the cup passed no special priestly class officiates. The universal priesthood of believers is seen functioning. In the Scripture there is no hint of one priest or minister officiating in a clerical role at the table.

This requires concerned worshipful hearts. No longer are Christians simply spectators watching a priest officiate at the altar. All are priests, singing, worshiping, adoring, exulting in God's love and grace, marveling at His Person.

The tone of worship is an accurate thermometer of the spiritual health of a fellowship. Spontaneous, genuine worship is difficult to imitate. The spiritual activity of the week is evident in the Word shared and prayers offered. When an assembly is healthy this is heaven on earth.

> Much incense is ascending
> Before the eternal throne,
> God graciously is bending
> To hear each feeble groan;
> To all our prayers and praises
> Christ adds His sweet perfume,
> And love the censer raises,
> These odors to consume.
> —Mary Bowley Peters

What are the benefits of this time? Certainly the Father and Son are pleased and honored. Gratitude for God's grace is not often expressed. Jesus asked, "Where are the nine?" Only one out of the ten lepers healed returned to thank Him and to praise God. Worship is almost a lost art today.

> Come, let us worship and bow down:
> Let us kneel before the Lord our Maker.
> For He is our God,
> And we are the people of His pasture
> And the sheep of His hand (Psa. 95:6,7)

The personal benefits of such worship are many. First, believers are moved to judge sin. Worship must be preceded by confession (Matt. 5:23, 24). How salutary for the body to know this cleansing and renewal. "But let a man examine himself and so let him eat and drink of the cup" (1 Cor. 11:28). Forgiveness and reconciliation should flow like a healing stream between individuals and families.

The breaking of bread is a proclamation of the cross (1 Cor. 11:26). Upon this death all salvation depends. Christ's death and resurrection are the basic message of the Church. Paul said, "But may it never be that I should boast, except in the cross of our Lord Jesus Christ" (Gal. 6:14). The breaking of bread is the Church boasting in the cross and reaffirming its centrality.

The first and great commandment is "You shall love the Lord your God with all your heart and with all your soul and with all your mind" (Matt. 22:37). The Lord's Supper calls upon the Church to love God. This act of supreme love and unselfishness, the death of Christ on the cross, is remembered afresh.

Such love should move the believer to the depths of his being. To meditate upon his love and death calls forth an answering response of love and devotion. "We love, because He first loved us" (1 John 4:19). To meditate on Christ offering Himself for sinners will move one to offer himself to God (Rom. 12:1, 2). It is a time of tender hearts and reconsecration to God.

To remember Christ's death also is to enter into His love for all of His children. Christians are one family, brothers and sisters, all sharing the Father's love and grace. It is to know the dying in self of hostility and bitterness and to know the warm, embracing, forgiving love of God poured out in our hearts (Rom. 5:5).

To remember Christ's death is to feel His great compassion for sinners. It is to hear Him say again, "Father, forgive them; for they do not know what they are doing" (Luke 23:34). It is to see His eyes brimming with love for those who spit in His face. It is to sense afresh the insanity and destructiveness of sin. It is to feel the dull ache of soul that He knew as He wept over the lost. It is to have one's love for the lost rekindled and to go out longing to tell others of the Savior's love and grace.

One could go on. The benefits of meditation on the cross with a company of God's people cannot be measured.

It is fitting then that an offering be taken in which God's people give freely and generously to the needs of God's work. Giving should be an enthusiastic expression of worship, a giving to God. "God loves a cheerful (hilarious) giver" (2 Cor. 9:7). The material gifts reflect the spiritual consecration of the redeemed.

The remembrance time has an eager, upward look. "You proclaim the Lord's death until He comes" (1 Cor. 11:26). The heart that has come to love the Savior longs to see His face and to hear His voice. The ecstasy of worship at the table will find fulfillment at the Lord's feet. "Come, Lord Jesus" is the cry of a worshiping church.

> Till He come we take the cup,
> As we at His table sup,
> Eye and heart are lifted up!
> We give Thee thanks, O Lord.
>
> For that coming here foreshown,
> For that day to man unknown,
> For the glory and the throne,
> We give Thee thanks, O Lord.
> —Horatius Bonar

8

CONCLUSION

What is your thinking now as a result of this study?

Many people are content just to drift along with the church group of which they are a part, never questioning, never doubting. Some also feel it is sacrilegious to question any of these matters. And yet in view of the wide diversity of doctrine and practice all cannot be right.

Does it matter whether we celebrate the Lord's Supper at all? Perhaps one can just think about Christ in the quietness of his own heart. But then there are those disquieting words, "This do in remembrance of Me." Did Christ mean what He said? If so, what of His words, "And why do you call Me Lord and do not what I say?" (Luke 6:46). Obedience to the Lord is always the fruit of love for the Lord. Let us quit saying that we love God when we reject His authority in our lives.

What about the frequency? Since the early Church universally remembered the Lord's death in the Lord's Supper every Sunday, does this make an impression? If under the guidance of Peter, John, Paul, and the other Apostles the churches made this a central part of their worship, do you feel their pattern should be emulated today? Were they not uniquely called and gifted to establish the Church and its practice?

Does not the practice of the churches in having spontaneous meetings (1 Cor. 14:26), open to the Spirit's prompting, make good sense. Does not this allow the priesthood of believers to function and encourage a fresh, vigorous expression of worship? Can Paul's instruction be improved? Does not Paul say with holy boldness, ". . . the things which I write to you are the Lord's commandment" (1 Cor. 14:37)?

Does not this weekly remembrance time nurture devotion to Christ? Can one remain unmoved if he sits for an hour or longer, contemplating the dying Christ? Will his love not be stirred as he hears others express their love and appreciation to the risen Savior?

Is it not a healthful thing for the body of Christians to examine their hearts and confess their sins before coming to the table? Is not tolerated sin the curse of churches today? Will not the contemplation of Christ's agony because of sin create a holy hatred of sin? Is not this a great need for Christians today?

Is not Christ's compassion for the lost written in blood on the cross? The worshiper should be moved to love as He loved. Does not the Church need to be stirred to evangelize those who sit in darkness?

Does not this time of worship fill one's heart with overflowing love for his brothers and sisters? How can one be bitter and unforgiving when Christ has forgiven him so much? Love in a church is a great proof of God's grace. Did not Jesus say, "By this all men will know that you are My disciples, if you have love for one another" (John 13:35)?

May this study move all of us to a greater commitment to worship and praise as we gather to remember our Lord Jesus in the breaking of bread.

> Amidst us our Beloved stands,
> And bids us view His pierced hands;
> Points to the wounded feet and side,
> Blest emblems of the crucified.

What food luxurious loads the board
When at His table sits the Lord!
The wine how rich, the bread how sweet,
When Jesus deigns the guests to meet!

If now with eyes defiled and dim,
We see the signs, but see not Him;
O may His love the scales displace,
And bid us see Him face to face!

Thou glorious Bridegroom of our hearts,
Thy present smile a neaven imparts!
O, lift the veil, if veil there be,
Let every saint Thy glory see!
                    —Charles H. Spurgeon

BIBLIOGRAPHY

Alford, Henry. *The Greek Testament*. Boston: Lee and Shepherd, 1874.

Bergendoff, Conrad and Nordgren, J. Vincent. *A Bible History*. Rock Island, Ill: Augustana, 1949

Broadus, John A. *The Gospel of Matthew*. Valley Forge: The Judson Press, 1886.

Bruce, F. F. *Answers to Questions*. Grand Rapids: Zondervan, 1972.

Bruce, F. F. *The Book of Acts*. Grand Rapids: Wm. B. Eerdmans, 1954.

Bruce, F. F. *The Gospel of John*. Grand Rapids: Wm. B. Eerdmans, 1983.

Calvin, John. *Institutes of the Christian Religion*. Grand Rapids: Wm. B. Eerdmans, 1962.

Darby, J. N. *Synopsis of the Books of the Bible*. New York: Loizeaux Bros.

Dictionary of the Apostolic Church. Edited by James Hastings. Edinburgh: T. & T. Clark, 1915.

Dictionary of Christ and the Gospels. Edited by James Hastings. Edinburgh: T. & T. Clark, 1906.

Dictionary of New Testament Theology. Edited by Colin Brown. Grand Rapids: Zondervan, 1975.

International Standard Bible Encyclopaedia. Edited by James Orr. Revised by M. G. Kyle. Grand Rapids: Wm. B. Eerdmans, 1946.

Latourette, Kenneth Scott. *A History of Christianity.* New York: Harper & Row, 1953.

Marshall, I. Howard. *The Gospel of Luke.* Grand Rapids: Wm. B. Eerdmans, 1978.

Plummer, Alfred. *An Exegetical Commentary to the Gospel According to Matthew.* London: Elliot Stock, 1910.

Schaff, Philip. *History of the Christian Church.* Grand Rapids: Wm. B. Eerdmans, reprinted 1970.

The Church, A Symposium. Edited by J. B. Watson. London: Pickering & Inglis, 1949.

The Expositors Greek Testament. Edited by W. Robertson Nicoll. Grand Rapids: Wm. B. Eerdmans, 1970.

The New Bible Dictionary. Edited by J. D. Douglas. Grand Rapids: Wm. B. Eerdmans, 1962.

Theological Dictionary of the New Testament. Edited by Gerhard Kittle. Translated by Geoffrey W. Bromiley. Grand Rapids: Wm. B. Eerdmans, 1964.

The Teaching of the Twelve Apostles. Edited by Roswell D. Hitchcock and Francis Brown. New York: Charles Scribners Son, 1885.